Portals of Love
The Collection

*For I know the plans I have for you,
declares the Lord, plans to prosper
you and not to harm you, plans
to give you hope and a future.*
—*Jeremiah 29:11*

Mourning as observed
through God's perspective.

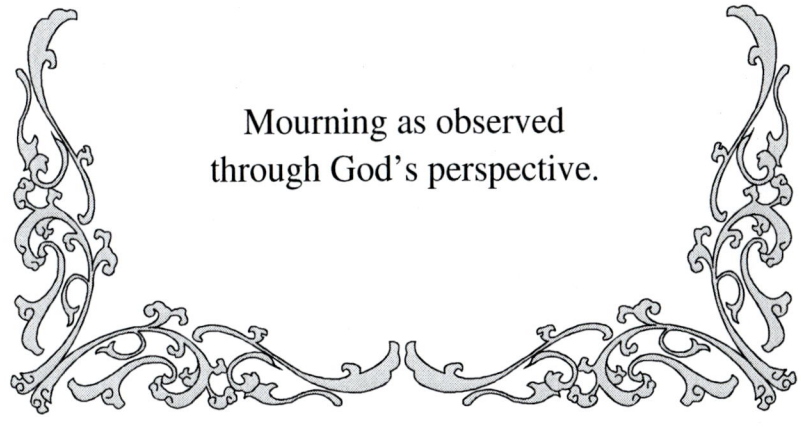

Also by Dennis R. Miller

Books
- *America's Heartbeat*
- *Tears of Love*
- *The Butterfly Home*
- *Upon A Time*

DVDs
- *Upon A Time*
- Portals of Love: The Collection
  - *Part I: Window to Heaven*
  - *Part II: Portal of Love*
  - *Part III: A Time to Die*
  - *Part IV: Born Again*

Portals of Love
The Collection

Dennis R. Miller

TEARS OF LOVE MINISTRY, INC.
Eau Claire, Wisconsin

A non-profit multi-media ministry serving to express God's love through sharing the compassion of Christ.

Copyright © 2010 by Dennis R. Miller
All rights reserved

Tears of Love Ministry, Inc.
S6150 Sundance Place
Eau Claire, Wisconsin 54701
Visit our website at http://tearsofloveministry.org

PORTALS OF LOVE: THE COLLECTION

Printed in the United States of America

Cover design and photographs by Dean L. Bauman, Videographer.

"A Time To Die." © 1997. Used by permission of the author, Dean L. Bauman. All rights reserved

"Together We'll Walk the Stepping Stones." © 1988. Used by permission of the author, Barbara Williams. All rights reserved

Unless stated differently, all scripture is from the HOLY BIBLE, NEW INTERNATIONAL VERSION®
© 1973, 1978, 1984 International Bible Society. Used by permission of Zondervan. All rights reserved

ISBN: 0-9661853-5-8

This book is dedicated to

Karen Joyce Miller

My wife, who, other than God,
has always been the best part of me.

Author's Note

THE BEST THINGS IN LIFE, I've learned, don't come easy. Rather, like climbing a mountain, the higher you go for a better view, the steeper and more difficult it becomes. So it was writing Portals of Love. Often I was plagued with feelings of self doubt and despair. I'd wonder, Why me, Lord? Who am I to do this?

Eventually, my outlook changed. Then I saw why the poor in spirit need to share what they've been through. Just as Christ was born in a lowly manger, we also need to reflect the humility and self-sacrifice of his life to help others envision the kingdom of heaven too.

While you read Portals of Love, I hope you will witness how God can use a broken layman so others may feel our Lord's compassion. Then, through his grace, may you see why it is most often when your eyes are moist with tears of love that God reveals his portals of love.

Dennis R. Miller
2010

Contents

Forward .... *i*
Preface .... *iii*

Introduction 1
PART I: Window to Heaven 7
PART II: Portal of Love 25
PART III: A Time to Die 51
PART IV: Born Again 67
Postlude 93

Epilogue 97
Notes 100

Forward

Dennis Miller is a man intimately acquainted with sorrow. His daughter was killed in a tragic accident and his journey through loss, grief, and mourning became the inspiration for *Portals of Love*, the book that you now hold in your hands. His soft-spoken and gentle manner is a testimony to the power of God's spirit and a witness to the work of restoration taking place in his life. I believe Dennis wants us to gain a more abundant love for God, ourselves, and our fellow man.

    As a young man I built race cars. Race car drivers appeared to me to be a tight-knit group who traveled and socialized together. Yet, if drivers were hurt in wrecks and consequently hospitalized, it seemed the other drivers would rarely visit. They would be supportive in every other way of their fallen comrade's families, but they almost seemed to avoid one-on-one contact in the hospital setting. These seemingly opposing actions and attitudes confused me, and I never understood why. I was reminded of this when Dennis spoke of the difference between grieving and mourning. Once I gave this some thought, I was able to better understand the reluctance of my race car buddies.

The book *Portals of Love* is written about a subject that too often is considered taboo. As we walk through life, all of us experience loss and grief on different levels ranging from the loss of a pet to the loss of a child. Many people tend to look at life as a battle. We do not allow anything superfluous to get in the way of our goals. We tend to deny or downplay our emotions. We certainly do not anticipate those devastating events that produce grief, especially the overwhelming kind that stops us in our tracks. Once I understood that I had not acknowledged my grief and, in fact, was avoiding it, I was able to move on to understanding the difference between grieving and mourning.

Therefore it seems to me there are two main audiences for this book: those who are in the grip of mourning an immediate tragedy and those who carry unresolved grief from a lifetime of losses. My council is to read and learn from Dennis' journey and to find your own portal of love.

—Reverend Michael G. Mills
Former rehabilitation director of Midwest Challenge

Preface

SIX MONTHS BEFORE SHE DIED, sixteen-year old Kimberly Joyce Miller, my daughter, gave me the book *Butterfly Kisses*. It contained pictures and tender thoughts shared between fathers and daughters. Then, I just skimmed it because I thought there would be plenty of time to read it.

Six months later, that special girl in my life was killed in a car accident.

Devastated, I went to a grief support center, where I begged for answers to survive. I was told that all whose hearts have been shattered by death and loss have stories they need to tell and they all start at the beginning. In time and after a lot of tears, I told my story through writing the book, *Tears of Love*.

As of now, I have written four books concerning bereavement. *Portals of Love* is book four. More than signifying grief, it expresses mourning through God's perspective.

A lot of people regard the words grieving and mourning as being synonymous; they are not. In fact, few words are more incorrectly interchangeable. Their misuse, like a smoke screen, causes many people to overlook the disparity between grieving and mourning and not to earnestly participate in getting well.

According to *Guidelines for Helping People*, a book written by W. H. Hunt, "Grief is the intense emotional suffering brought on by a significant personal loss. The most obvious example of grief is associated with the death of a loved one."[1] While the word grief is the noun or name of this intense emotional suffering, mourning, like a verb, is the act of expressing our grief to the outside world.[2] In other words, it is the process of externalizing the intense sorrow from within the heart.

I learned to differentiate between these words years ago. The lesson occurred from a coworker about a month after Kimmy passed away. When he approached me, he had been sober for a long time, but such was not always the case. Years earlier his wife had committed suicide. Though his voice was steady as he told me what had happened, I could still sense his helplessness and frustration.

"I couldn't take it." He looked me in the eye. "For ten years I hid myself in a bottle. But while the drinking took the edge off the pain, it also stopped me from mourning. I wasted ten years to just grieving and drinking before I started to move on with my life."

After he left, I cried for us both. Some tears were for my mourning. Others were for him who, in his own way, had tried to tell me not to get trapped in a similar snare.

None of us are immune to sorrow. Though each of us will grieve, not all of us will mourn. Besides alcohol and drugs, often our outlook, the way we view grief, keeps us from mourning. For example:

MYTHS AND FACTS ABOUT GRIEF

> **Myth**: The pain will go away faster if you ignore it.
> **Fact**: Trying to ignore your pain or keep it from surfacing will only make it worse in the long run. For real healing it is necessary to face your grief and actively deal with it.
> **Myth**: It's important to "be strong" in the face of loss.
> **Fact**: Feeling sad, frightened, or lonely is a normal reaction to loss. Crying doesn't mean you are weak. You don't need to "protect" your family or friends by putting on a brave front. Showing your true feelings can help them and you.[3]
> —*Bertolon Center for Grief & Healing*

Another reason why we do not mourn is because we feel abandoned by God. We think that if he cared our hearts would not be branded by grief. Again, this not uncommon response to loss, like a myth, is wrong. God does care.

> People are like stained glass windows; they
> sparkle and shine when the sun is out, but when
> the darkness sets in, their true beauty is revealed only if
> there is a light within.[4]
> —*Elisabeth Kubler-Ross, M.D.*

Death is a common cause for the loss of innocence. When it invades our lives, our souls become lost and cloaked in darkness. Real grief, the type that breaks our hearts and blotches out our hope and joy, leaves a black stain on us.

At first family and friends try to help. They patted me on the back, gave me hugs, and listened. Later, going to the grief support center and being with others who had experienced the same feelings as me, helped me. Moreover, they gave me a safe place to express my pain by talking about the loss of my daughter. Yet, no matter where I was in expressing my grief, only God removed the darkness within.

Like members of Alcoholics Anonymous, we need to take step two and come "to believe that a power greater than ourselves [can] restore us to sanity."[5]

I am aware that my belief might seem empty to those devastated by grief. Still, we can't lose faith or forget that God is a bereaved parent too.

In the summer of 2003, I worked with a group of bereaved parents and community members to create the Angel of Hope Memorial Garden in Eau Claire, Wisconsin. The shape of the garden was designed to resemble hands in prayer. Its focal point is the Angel of Hope sculpture that was first introduced by author Richard Paul Evans in his book, *The Christmas Box*.

The mission of the memorial garden is to provide inspiration, healing, and enlightenment. I believe the angel has helped many parents who have endured the loss of a child. As I stand before the Angel of Hope, the statue is a reminder to me of God's spiritual messengers and how they, his angels, are often depicted as a bridge between heaven and earth. With a suggestion of reverence, the angel's face is tilted slightly upward toward the stars. Her hands point down with open palms as if wanting to disclose what God has said.

Like one of the many oak leaves falling softly to the ground, I, like most who believe in angels, hear in the still pool of my consciousness, the message:

*Blessed are they who mourn,
for they will be comforted.*
—*Matthew 5:4*

It is a terrible thing to observe hopelessness in one alive. He or she seems like a corpse, a body without life. When Jesus said, "Blessed are they that mourn," *blessed* to him meant to experience hope and joy again. Thus, while grieving is the price we pay for having loved, mourning is the act of redemption we do by expressing this love. When sharing God's love with others, Christ becomes our vision, his presence our hope within. To the dark world of deep grief, we who mourn express the greatest light. As the Reverend Simon Stephens, founder of The Compassionate Friends, said:

HOPE

It is the gift of ***hope*** which reigns supreme in the attributes of The Compassionate Friends. ***Hope*** that all is not lost. ***Hope*** that life can still be worth living and meaningful. ***Hope*** that the pain of loss will become less acute and, above all else, the ***hope*** that we do not walk alone, that we are understood. The gift of ***hope*** is the greatest gift that we can give to those who mourn.[6]

The best way to witness to others is simply to relate what God has done in your life. Today, instead of a heart that is lost, I have a heart for the lost. That's why I have written *Portals of Love*.

Just as looking at sorrow from God's perspective gives me hope and joy, so my faith gives me the strength to face my pain, mourn for my loss, and continue—I pray that this outlook on mourning will do the same for you.

Portals of Love
The Collection

Introduction

And the earth was without form, and void, and darkness was upon the face of the deep. And the spirit of God moved upon the faces of the water. And God said, let there be light; and there was light.

—*Genesis 1:2-3*

THE GENESIS OF MAN'S AWARENESS of grief has regretfully lagged far behind that of our creation. In fact, even now for many people, it is a closeted experience. Like an ostrich burying its head in the sand, those who are grieving the loss of a loved one often keep their sorrow buried in the recesses of their hearts. Compounding this problem is that they feel unsupported and uncomforted by their families, friends, and even their church. The truth is most people do not understand what someone whose heart has been broken is going through because they have not experienced such grief yet themselves. Once I was like them too.

When I recall how I used to be, my thoughts turn to my

daughter Kimmy. We had so much in common. Like me, Kimmy was strong-willed, persistent, and very compassionate. And we loved to play ping-pong. Before she was big enough to hit the ball over the net, I used to stand her on a chair to play. When she grew taller, we became passionate competitors.

We also shared a genuine love for writing. Whether it was a journal, poem, or a book, writing seemed to be our natural way of expression. When she was sixteen, Kimmy showed me a poem she had written. I was overcome by her style and literary promise, and I hoped that someday we would venture together on a joint authorship project.

On January 22, 1999, my dream was shattered. Kimmy and her passenger, Lalan Ho, were killed in a car accident. They were only sixteen and fifteen years old.

Before Kimmy's death, I considered myself a strong person. The truth is, until then, I did not know real grief.

Rick Warren wrote in his book, *The Purpose Driven Life*, "God never wastes a hurt! In fact, your greatest ministry will most likely come out of your greatest hurt."[7] I agree.

After Kimmy's death, I founded the Tears of Love Ministry. I wanted to express God's love through sharing the compassion of Christ.

The event that inspired me to write *Portals of Love* began on January 24, 1999. It was on a Sunday, the day before Kimmy's funeral. Though I had prayed repeatedly that Kimmy was okay and at peace with her Lord, I was not consoled. Karen and I went to church, hoping to see that our prayers were answered. Again, we were not comforted and because the grief became too unbearable, we had to leave.

We stopped to pick up the Sunday paper. Back home, sitting in the living room, I began to read our daughter's obituary.

> Kimberly Joyce miller, age 16, of S6150 Sundance Place, Eau Claire, passed away on Friday, January 22, 1999. She attended Little Red Elementary School and was currently a junior at Eau Claire Memorial High School. Kimmy was a member of the Eau Claire Ski Sprites and she enjoyed playing softball and ping-pong...

I could not read any further. As a man who grew up believing husbands should have all the answers and that fathers should be able to fix anything, I felt like a failure.

The anguish in my heart reminded me of the child's fairy tale *Humpty Dumpty*. Like the king's servants, I could not put Humpty Dumpty together again. I was unable to explain, let alone fix, the hole in my heart. Again, my grief became unbearable. I put down the newspaper. Wanting to hide the coming tears, I turned towards the window. In what felt like my darkest moment, everything I could do had been done. The funeral arrangements were all taken care of.

During this futile time, when I felt there was nothing more I could do, the Lord became a light unto me. The greatest aspiration he showed me was that we can acquire spiritual understanding. As a child, the spirit of God was puzzling to me. Even when I was older, it seemed too mysterious and beyond my comprehension.

Likewise, I could not interpret love or the lack of it back then either. In high school it was customary for the seniors on the football team to invite their father to the last home game. They called it Father's Day. Back then, because I felt my stepfather did not care that much about me and would not want to go, I did not ask him to attend. Years later, after he passed away, I discovered that I had been very wrong. We were cleaning out his junk drawer, which is where a lot of men place their keepsakes, and to my surprise we found the ticket for Father's Day that the school had mailed to him. This man, who had never said "I love you" to me for all those years, had kept the invitation with his keepsakes.

Before Kimmy's death, I had cried only a handful of times. One of them was then, when I deeply regretted not inviting my stepdad to Father's Day.

Now, while staring out the frosted picture window in my living room, I wondered, *Did Kimmy know how much I loved her?*

Unlike the wasted years it took me to know that my stepdad loved me, I was blessed. Through the window I experienced the Spirit of God. As in Genesis 1:2-3, "there was light." Within its brilliance and comfort, I recalled the last conversation Kimmy and I had shared. I had worked the midnight shift. By 7:30 A.M. I was home and in bed when Kimmy came in and asked me if she could take my car to school.

"Okay," I answered, "but drive carefully. The roads are

a little bad." "Yeah, yeah," she responded, sounding like a typical teenager, as if I cared more for my car than her. "It's not the car I'm worried about," I told her. "It's you. I love you."

More than answering my question, my last three words to my daughter were a blessing; one that I will forever thank God for. From his act of grace, I was inspired to write *Window to Heaven*. By his grace I was moved to go to church alone. Not wanting to look conspicuous, I sat in the back pew, never knowing, yet always expecting a wave of grief to push me to tears. It was during these times, when my eyes were moist, that God revealed his portals of love to me.

After writing *Window to Heaven*, I saw that love is the connection between grieving and becoming whole again after a great loss. The concept that grieving is about loving inspired me to write *Part II: Portal of Love*.

While writing part two, it became clear to me that to love God's way requires us to break down the walls that we hide behind and to open our hearts. Sadly, many people are too fearful to do so. To show others how love can overcome fear, I wrote *Part III: A Time to Die*.

Nothing exemplifies love as much as God's grace. From his love my spirit has been rejuvenated and healed. Wanting to share this transforming power, I wrote *Part IV: Born Again*.

Each of the parts of this book, like four sections of a circle, stands alone as an uplifting arch. Together, the parts form a ring that substantiates God's unconditional and eternal love for us.

———

In my last moment with Kimmy, when I was tired and wanted to go to sleep, I could have argued with her and maybe said something I would later regret. None of us are perfect. More than any friend, God knows the good and bad in each of us. Yet even from my impure and corrupt heart, he allowed my last three words to be…"I love you."

Today, years later, my eyes continue to moisten, but with tears of humble gratitude as I remember my final words to Kimmy.

Reverend Simon Stephens said, "Those of us who have worked through our grief and found there is a future—are the ones who must meet others in the valley of darkness and bring them to the light."[8] We who know what the newly bereaved are going through must share our new hope and joy with them.

Grieving is about loving. Just as how well we mourn hinges similarly on how much we believe God loves us. For those who grieve, may you experience through *Portals of Love* mourning from God's perspective.

PART I

Window to Heaven

—Angel of Hope Memorial Garden, Eau Claire, Wisconsin

*"Send forth your light and your truth,
let them guide me."*

—*Psalm 43:3*

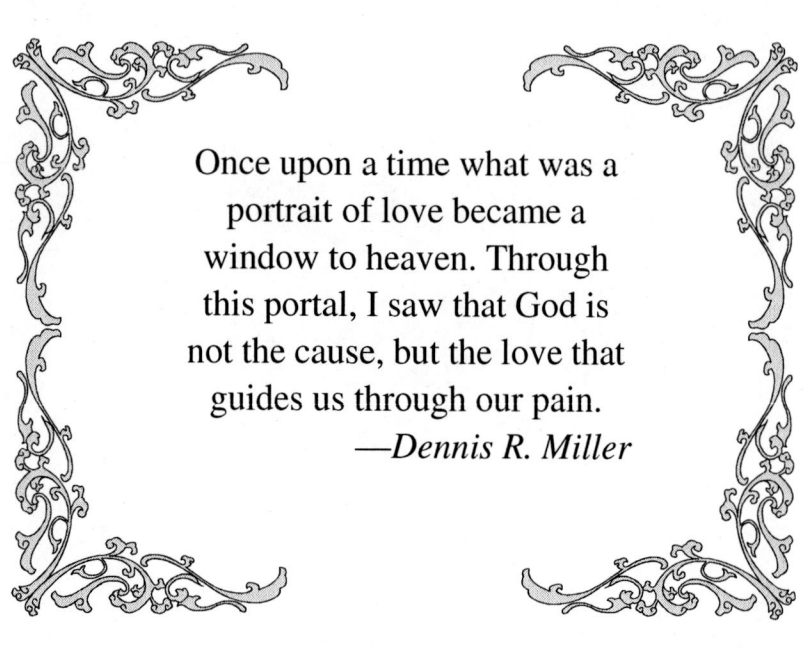

Once upon a time what was a portrait of love became a window to heaven. Through this portal, I saw that God is not the cause, but the love that guides us through our pain.
—*Dennis R. Miller*

Window to Heaven

THE MISSION FOCUS FOR THE Tears of Love Ministry comes from Second Corinthians 1:3-4.

> *Praise be to God and Father of our Lord Jesus Christ, The Father of compassion and the God of all comfort, Who comforts us in all our troubles, So that we can comfort those in any trouble with the comfort we ourselves have received from God.*
> —*2 Corinthians 1:3-4*

Many of us have experienced faith-filled moments. Sometimes these special moments are referred to as thin places; awe-inspiring instances where the world of the spiritual and the world of the physical meet. For me, such a moment occurred on January 24, 1999. It was on a Sunday, the day before my daughter Kimmy's funeral.

On this cold, sunny wintry day, I was sitting on the davenport at home. Turning toward the frosted picture window with tear-filled eyes, my gaze lifted to the distant hills. The light that shone from the horizon was the most glorious sight that I had ever encountered. Though the love and warmth that came from this moment cannot be easily conveyed into words, what happened was very real! Cradled within the light, I knew I was in the presence of someone far greater than myself and was moved to share this inspiration and wonder with others.

> *Grief* is the normal reaction to death and loss.
>
> At some time most of us will experience our life becoming painfully *tilted* due to some traumatic *loss*.
>
> However, whenever a door is *closed*, God *opens* a window.
>
> It is with a grateful heart that we praise God for opening a window to heaven.

God is not the cause but the love that guides us through our pain from death and loss.

Heavenly Father, I believe that the scripture passages within your Holy Bible contain your divine answers to our deepest needs. May all who are grieving, fearful, and lost be moved by the compassion of Christ to seek your love. Thank you, Lord. Amen.

The passage from this portal of love leads us to heal God's way.

Even though I walk through the valley of the shadow of death, I will fear no evil, for you are with me; Your rod and your staff, they comfort me.

—*Psalm 23:4*

Before my daughter Kimmy was killed in a car accident, I believed I was a strong person. I could have counted on one hand the number of times I had cried. After her death, well, I just could not count that high. Though crying could not bring back my daughter, tears of love did bring me back. I found a faithful Father whose love can guide us through the shadow of death.

Years ago, Barbara Williams, a nurse at a hospital in Fort Wayne, Indiana, comforted a couple who had just lost their child. The next day Barbara, a bereaved parent herself, wrote the following poem.

TOGETHER WE'LL WALK THE STEPPING STONES

Come, take my hand, the road is long. We must travel by stepping stones. No, you're not alone. I'll go with you. I know the road well; I've been there. Don't fear the darkness. I'll be with you. We must take one step at a time. But remember, we may have to stop awhile. It is a long way to the other side and there are many obstacles.

We have many stones to cross. Some are bigger than others—SHOCK, DENIAL, and ANGER to start. Then comes GUILT, DESPAIR, and LONELINESS. It's a hard road to travel, but it must be done. It's the only way to reach the other side.

Come, slip your hand in mine. What? Oh, yes, it's strong. I've held so many hands like yours. Yes, mine was one time small and weak like yours. Once, you see, I had to take someone's hand in order to take the first step. Oops! You've stumbled. Go ahead and cry. Don't be ashamed. I understand. Let's wait here awhile and get your breath. When you're stronger we'll go on, one step at a time. There's no need to hurry.

Say, it's nice to hear you laugh. Yes, I agree, the memories you shared are good. Look we're halfway there now; I can see the other side. It looks so warm and sunny. Oh have you noticed? We're nearing the last stone and you're standing alone. And look, your hands, you've let go of mine, and we've reached the other side.

But wait. Look back. Someone is standing there. They are alone and want to cross the stepping stones. I better go; they need my help. What? Are you sure? Why, yes; I'll wait. Yes, I agree, it's your turn, my friend, to help someone else across the stepping stones.

—*Barbara Williams*

Barbara wrote to me after I asked for consent to use her poem, and I would like to share part of her note with you.

She said: "I am humbled by your interest in the poem and appreciate your kind words. My mission in the poem is to help and ease some of the grief of losing a child and to let others know there is help, even though the road is long. In life there is no greater loss then to lose a child."

Thank you, Barbara.

Heartbreaking grief that leads us into denial can leave us emotionally blind. I was that way the first time I read Barbara's poem. Lost in the depths of my sorrow, I reached out, groping like someone who could not see. Indeed, God has blessed Barbara and everyone else who has read her poem and felt God's presence.

Just like fingerprints, each of us has our own story and way of dealing with grief. The telling of your story is an essential part of the healing process. Like peeling away the layers of an onion, whenever you recognize the truth about your loss, you strip off a layer of grief. Too many people never tell their story. Instead, at the risk of losing themselves, they keep it buried in the recess of their hearts.

Through people like Barbara Williams, God often touches us. By his grace may our Savior's gospel of hope and life continue to lead us.

There are *five* stages to grief as we learned from Dr. Elisabeth Kubler-Ross, a Swiss-born American psychiatrist, who pioneered this concept in her book, *On Death and Dying*.[9] Since Kimmy's death, I have experienced all of them.

Each stage pertains to a specific chapter in our stories.

To comfort others with the comfort my family and I have received, I would like to share my personal story.

Besides offering solace, may it help others with broken hearts cross *the stepping stones*.

Denial

THE FIRST CHAPTER is *Denial*.

When the detective told me that my daughter Kimmy was dead, the news kicked my legs out from under me. Later, when calling family members, I sank even deeper into shock and denial. I repeated over and over what the detective had told me.

I said it, but I did not believe it.

> **Has the shock of your loss worn off yet?**
>
> **Are you ready to walk toward the far side and be healed?**

Lord, here is my hand reaching out to you. Let your love be my guide and strength as I begin my journey to the other side. Amen.

Anger

THE SECOND CHAPTER is *Anger*.

Anger is the grip of grief. No other emotion holds you so firm. It is a natural consequence of losing someone or something you value.

Shortly after Kimmy's death, I was shopping at Shopko and everything seemed normal. People were talking and laughing in the checkout lines as if nothing had happened.

How could they not know the world was not the same now?

Upset, I wanted to shout, "Kimmy is dead!" But then I realized their lives had not changed, only my small world was tilted and would never be the same again.

Though we as a society do not process anger very well, it is important that we learn to accept and deal with these intense feelings. Anger tells us that something is terribly wrong.

Bargaining

THE THIRD CHAPTER is *Bargaining*.

This phase of grief is often the briefest of all the stages. It is the final effort to hold onto what is important and to avoid all the pain, guilt, and sorrow. But God has given us a way to overcome. He wants us to process our grief. Jesus spoke of a promise in Matthew 5:4.

> *Blessed are they that mourn for they shall be comforted.*
> —*Matthew 5:4*

When I was a child, I noticed my stepfather spent a lot of time staring out the kitchen window. I did not understand why. Today I do.

To you who stare out windows, God's promise grants us permission to mourn, offers us comfort when we do, and finally gives us hope.

Depression

THE FOURTH CHAPTER is *Depression.*

Depression occurs when we finally stop hiding and allow ourselves to experience the sadness of our loss.

Three weeks after Kimmy died was St. Valentine's Day. Parking the car near her grave, I stepped out, carrying a Valentine's card. The closer Kimmy's headstone loomed, the slower I walked. Its stark reality wrenched tears from me that blurred my vision. I encircled her grave, crying like a wounded animal.

The phrase *like an animal* reminds me of a man people called Oneida Joe. He was a hobo who roamed the country in boxcars during the Great Depression. As a ten-year-old child, I only knew him by sight when he walked the railroad tracks behind our house. Then, people called him a bum. He didn't have any friends, and his only companion was a Heinz fifty-seven mutt. They looked alike. Both were skinny and their thin hair, like their life, bore snarls.

When Oneida Joe died, the county buried him. There was no marker at his grave, only his doleful companion lying faithfully upon the fresh mound.

Like Oneida Joe's dog, I was lying in sadness, unable

to grasp what to do after Kimmy's death.

We live in a microwave society that wants everything fast and easy, even grief. A newspaper ran a survey that asked people how long they felt it took to mourn the loss of a loved one. The response was forty-eight hours to two weeks.[10]

According to the American Academy of Family Physicians, "you'll probably start to feel better in six to eight weeks. The whole process can last anywhere from six months to four years."[11] From my own experience I would agree.

On St. Valentine's Day I was so consumed by grief, I felt like the earth had opened up and swallowed everything I cherished. "My God! My God!" I cried. "Will I ever stop hurting? Why do I have to know such grief?"

One antidote for depression is to meditate on God's goodness to his people. After a lot of tears, time, and reflection, the depth of God's love became overwhelming to me. It was as if I was peering through a window to heaven. In a profound way, the experience gave me a glimpse of God as a bereaved father and what it meant for him to give up his son for us. As one who would have given up his own life to save his child, at last I understood what John said:

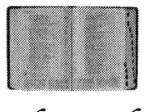

> *For God so loved the world that he gave his one and only Son that whoever believes in him shall not perish but have eternal life.*
>
> —John 3:16

Seven hundred and fifty years before Jesus was born, the prophet Isaiah predicted his crucifixion. This prophecy has been fulfilled for more than two thousand years now. Yet even today, Isaiah's words continue to make whole our lives whenever we see the cross.

> *Surely he hath borne our griefs, and carried our sorrows.*
> —*Isaiah 53:4*

Acceptance

THE FIFTH AND FINAL CHAPTER of grieving is *Acceptance*.

It is not easy to accept the rhythm of life as it really is, especially when you lose someone very precious to you. Yet, like miracles, acceptance can occur.

After finally comprehending John 3:16, I carried God's love with me the next time I went to the cemetery. Approaching my daughter's grave, a lone sparrow perched on a high line stared towards me. Again, I circled Kimmy's grave and tears came to my eyes. But this time, standing at the base of the grave, something marvelous happened. First, I noticed that the little sparrow had flown away. Then I felt a strange stirring within me, a misty consciousness, a sense of something remembered. It was as if I had come back to life after being dead.

Love does not die.

Realizing that only my daughter's body rested in this earth, no longer was I like an animal that could only lie upon its sadness. Like the sparrow that flew away, so had Kimmy's spirit to be with her Lord.

Conclusion

SOMETIME AGO I READ AN ARTICLE in a newsletter that quoted Dr. Gerald Jampolsky, the founder of the Center for Attitudinal Healing. He said that "healing is letting go of the fearful child so many of us carry inside and awaking to the innocent child who has always been within us."[12]

Besides agreeing with him, after looking through a window to heaven, I believe that just as grieving is about loving, so is healing. It is about loving a loved one who has passed on and loving yourself to go on with your life. First and foremost, however, it is about loving God and accepting his most eternal promise that just as the love in our hearts will not die, neither will our loved ones who believed in him.

Heavenly Father, as a child who is hurt would cry out, may all who are grieving come to you. Thank you for opening a window to heaven to reveal your wonderful gospel of hope and life. Through the compassion of Christ, the Creator of the world, may we continue to witness your love whenever—"Creation Calls." Amen.

PART II

Portal of Love

—Angel of Hope Memorial Garden, Eau Claire, Wisconsin

*"The Lord will fulfill his purpose for me;
Your love, O Lord, endures forever."*
—Psalm 138:8

Because God's love will
endure forever, the concept
that grieving is about loving
discloses that God will
fulfill his purpose in us.
—*Dennis R. Miller*

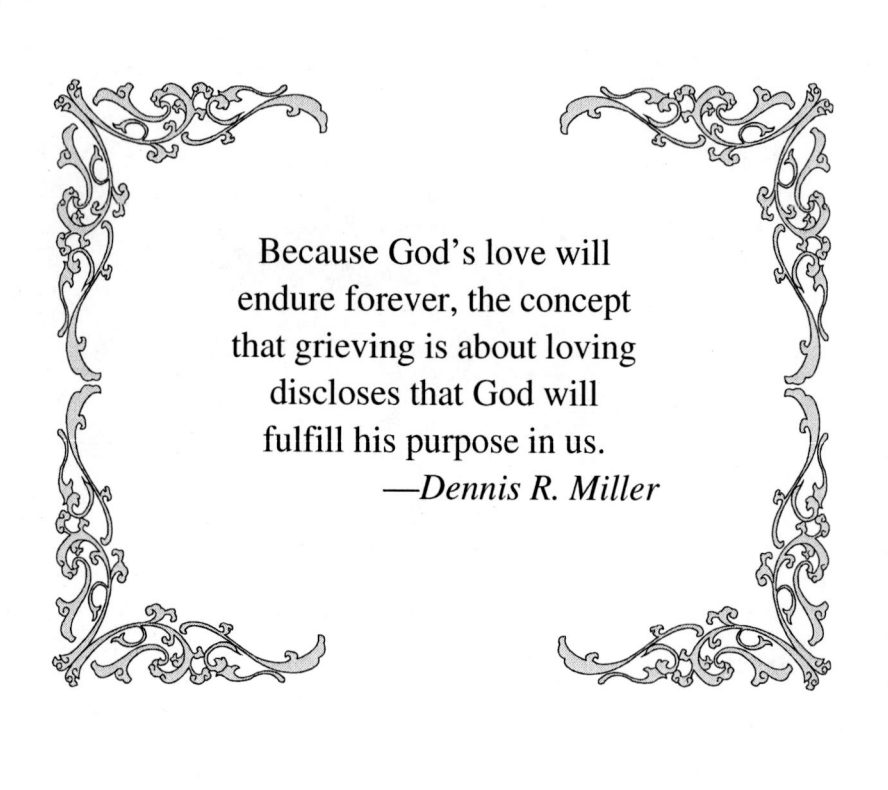

Portal of Love

THOUGH WE IN OUR HIGH-TECH CULTURE want everything fast and easy, healing from loss does not come as quickly as we would like. It took fourteen months after my daughter's death before I realized love does not die. Throughout this period, the inspiration I received from feeling God's presence the day before Kimmy's funeral helped sustained me.

The spirit that filled me was one of peace and inspiration, love and warmth. Churches have long spoken of the shining light that I experienced that day as the divine light, the light of light, the eternal light that shines in every heart. As a lifeline, that evidence of God's grace helped me and pulled my heart toward the portal of love that God offered.

The key to healing God's way is knowing his love. During my darkest hour, God's blessing made a way where none seemed to be.

Heavenly Father, thank you for your unfailing grace. When we are confused

and lost, it guides us and makes a way for us where none seems to be. Through faith in you may we observe your window of grace as a portal of love, a way for us to continue. Amen.

So often in life our plans waiver as we see our hopes and dreams crumble because of loss and death. And yet our grief can often lead to new awakenings of our hearts.

Because I grew up as an illegitimate child in the 1940s, being a good father was especially important to me. After my daughter's death, I was overcome with sorrow. Feelings of guilt plagued me and caused me to question whether Kimmy knew how much I had loved her.

With our hearts consumed with grief, my wife, Karen, and I struggled to find the right words for Kimmy's headstone. I wanted something like "Dwelling in the House of the Lord." It satisfied me, but not Karen. Disheartened, we began looking again. A few days later, Karen wrote something down. "What do you think of this?" she asked and handed me a piece of paper.

Today, Karen's words arch between two burst crosses on Kimmy's monument like a rainbow. More than just assuring us that Kimmy is okay, it has become a comfort to us, too, as we strive to go forward.

> At the end of the rainbow,
> the mountain touches the sky
> and God's holding my hand.

Through our Lord's compassion, God reveals his love.

May we forever open our hearts and welcome him with outstretched arms.

> *I am the gate; whoever enters through me will be saved. He will come in and go out, and find pasture.*
> —John 10:9

No matter what your spiritual beliefs may be, grieving can be complicated, challenging, and overwhelming. At some time during the first four stages of grief: denial, anger, bargaining, and depression, most of us will think we are okay and can handle the pain. But then tomorrow comes and we feel our whole world shaken once more, making the grieving process seem endless.

In my experience how we cope with suffering depends a lot on the type of relationship we have with God. Eighty-three percent of our population claim to be Christian,[13] yet so many of us who are grieving question if we can ever find purpose and meaning again. While it has been God's divine function to actively pursue a relationship with us whom he has created, far too many of us have been very slow to react or refused to respond at all.

One of the most important figures in the development of western Christianity, Saint Augustine, believed that the highest human faculty is love; and that love, not the intellect, is the standard from which God classifies us.[14] In John 13:35, the Lord said, "By this all men will know that you are my disciples, if you love one another." Since we describe our relationships through love, as pilgrims predestined to conform to the likeness of Christ, love therefore defines our relationship with God.

For a Christian, God's word is the authority on life and death. The Bible categorizes us into four groups: dead Christians, bound Christians, free Christians, and complete Christians and offers us a road map to help us grow into what God intended us to be.

In Greek, the language the New Testament was first written in, there are four words that express four different forms of love: eros, storge, philo, and agape. In a good and happy marriage, all four of these exist. For example, King Solomon affirms the sanctity of marriage by describing how his bride loves him.

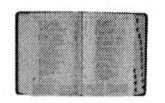

> *Place me like a seal over your heart,*
> *like a seal on your arm:*
> *For love is as strong as death,*
> *its jealousy unyielding as the grave.*
> *It burns like a blazing fire,*
> *like a mighty flame.*
> *Many waters cannot quench love:*
> *rivers cannot wash it away.*
> *If one were to give*
> *all the wealth of his house for love,*
> *it would be utterly scorned.*
> —Song of Songs 8:6-7

Indeed, there were no secrets between Solomon and his wife. Because they were both devoted and connected to their relationship, their love grew after their wedding night.

Similarly, all four loves should be in our relationship with God. More than to just comfort us in tragedy, God is fully devoted and committed to us. He wants to help us love others as much as he loves us. In the process of mourning, his love offers us a way to go on where none seems to be and helps us to heal.

In John 14:6, Jesus said: "I am the way and the truth and the life." As the truth, Jesus is the reality of all God's promises.

How are God's promises fulfilled in your heart?

The way we interpret suffering depends a lot on our perspective of love. Consequently, before we can move forward and begin to heal God's way, it is necessary that we first distinguish what stage or stages of love we currently reside in. Since only God's truth can set us free, we will begin by discussing each of the four stages of love. Within each form of love, we shall then highlight:

1. The kind of relationship it corresponds to between God and us.
2. The type of Christian that exists in it.
3. And why such Christians deal with suffering the way they do.

Then, when we are aware of and confess the level of

love we have been functioning in, God, according to his word, will lead us on to become a fully alive follower of Christ. In II Corinthians 1:5, it is said: "For just as the suffering of Christ flows over into our lives, so also through Christ our comfort overflows." With this hope genuinely prevalent in our hearts, we shall heal.

Eros Love

THE FIRST GROUP THE BIBLE separates us into is dead Christians. It is made up entirely of people who dwell in the stage of love called *eros*.

Eros love is the passionate or romantic form of love that displays an attraction and physical affection between a man and a woman. When combined with the other three loves in marriage, it is like the cherry on a sundae, a topping of pure joy. Alone, however, eros love is very unfulfilling. Like an alcoholic for whom one drink is too many and a million is never enough, those who only seek this kind of love become a slave to their addictions and the world.

When most people hear of someone lost in eros love, they imagine sexual bliss. Few consider such a person as someone who has deprived himself or herself of a way to God.

In my early Christian life, I never went to church by myself because it made me feel too alone. Instead, I found companionship at bars. To excuse myself for not going to church, I would blame the people who attended regularly as being too cliquish. Though some were, the truth is that most of the feelings that prevented me from living a Christian life stemmed from my childhood hang-ups. Later, when I was married and had a family, we attended church; yet still, I often felt out of place, like I did not belong. I was a dead Christian like the following key verse from Revelation describes.

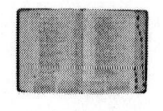

> *I know your works, that you have a name, that you are alive, but you are dead.*
>
> —*Revelation 3:1*

The Apostle John wrote this verse to the wealthy church of Sardis, one of the seven churches of Asia Minor. Instead of being concerned about others, the Christians in Sardis had no passion anymore for the things of God. John's message warned the people to be watchful and alive to what was going on in their lives because they were suffering from spiritual death like many people do today. According to Dr. M. Scott Peck, a noted psychiatrist and Christian author, dead Christians make up 20 percent of the population.[15]

For those who dwell only in eros love, the kind of relationship they share with God resembles that between a slave and his master. When I was a dead Christian, I found nothing positive about death. Like a wounded animal, suffering and loss filled me with an intangible fear, something I could not touch or understand.

Is your life stuck in the world as a slave to eros love?

Or are you making God's love a part of what and who you are?

Heavenly Father, I confess that too often I've failed to remember the real issues of my life that brought me to Christ. While I realize there is nothing I can do to make me worthy of you, I pray that by your grace, you will bless me. As one who hungers and thirsts for righteousness, free me from being a slave to the world so I may become your servant. Amen.

Storge Love

THE SECOND GROUP OF CHRISTIANS is bound Christians. They dwell primarily in the stage of love called s*torge*.

Storge love is family love such as a hug or a kiss between a parent and child or between siblings. It can also refer to the comfort provided to extended families like those who bond together in the military, gangs, and churches. Because families are smaller, more broken up, and spread out today, people often choose these alternatives for the supportive structures they offer.

When most people hear of someone committed only to storge love, they imagine a person very loving and family oriented. Here again, however, people who are bound solely to this form of love are depriving themselves of the greater love of God by serving the world rather than God.

In my early Christian life, I noticed that many people in my church appeared to constantly compare themselves to others, their self-worth dependant on winning, popularity, and power. Regrettably, like so many other churchgoers, I was also in bondage to my sins. I had chosen to dwell in storge love and to worship God according to what I believed and not God's word. Such an outlook becomes a self-imposed trap for bound Christians because their will is tied to the allurement of sin.

We can only serve one master and without a greater sense of God, our self-worth does not come from glorifying God but from the world. The following key verse from Galations describes what God wants for us.

> *It is for freedom that Christ has set us free. Stand firm, then, and do not let yourselves be burdened by a yoke of slavery.*
> —*Galatians 5:1*

This verse was written by the Apostle Paul to the four churches in Galatia located in southern Turkey. At the time, A.D. 49, a pressing controversy existed between the converts, Jewish Christians, and the Gentile Christians. The Jewish Christians believed that the Gentiles must obey Jewish law to be saved. In Galatians, Paul shows why the law is no longer needed and how we are saved by faith.

So it is for us today. By our faith in Christ that saves us from a life of slavery, we have been liberated to choose what we will. Bound Christians who continue to dwell in storge love, however, find their relationship with God is similar to that of a bonded or hired servant since they have remained tied to their sins. They handle suffering with great difficulty because of their low self-esteem, and they often view death with a sense of terror and a lack of control. Unless they change their relationship with God, they could become angry and cut off from others.

As a bound Christian, the loss of Kimmy was like a

near death experience for me. Never had I felt so helpless and utterly alone. My heart was breaking. I knew without help the emotions bottled up inside me would implode. A member of my church told me about The Healing Place, a grief support center. Though I had never heard of it before, I am glad I went there. By reaching out for help, I did not become bitter or isolated. Instead, I found the only relief that could overcome my loss…God's love.

Besides allowing me to vent my sorrows and tell my story, two other things at my first group meeting helped me. First, I realized that I was not alone. Until Kimmy's death, I had not known how devastating grief could be. In my mind I knew that others had suffered as I did, yet in my heart I felt detached. Not until I saw the tears in others' eyes and heard their tragic stories did I see that I was not alone, that others too had been engulfed by their grief.

Second, going to The Healing Place helped me immediately because it opened my heart to the fact that others had suffered severe losses too and survived. When you are in so much pain, you draw comfort any way you can. When a mother told me her story about her son's death ten years earlier, I knew that she understood the depths of my grief. It was not so much her words that drew me to her, but her eyes. Even after so long, you could still sense her tears when she shared her story.

Though it was not easy going to The Healing Place, the fact is I had no choice. If I had not gone, I know I would have died, whether from my broken heart or by numbing my pain with alcohol or drugs. One way or another, I feel my life would have ended without their help.

Please, for whatever reason your heart is breaking, do

not turn away from getting help if you need it. You are not alone.

Helen Keller wrote: "Once I knew only darkness and stillness...my life was without past or future...but a little word from the fingers of another fell into my hand that clutched at emptiness, and my heart leaped to the rapture of living."[16]

Helen Keller's teacher Anne Sullivan is remembered as "a miracle worker."[17]

> **Who will be the miracle worker in your life?**
>
> **Who will help you make the connection between grieving and loving?**

When we grow through grief God's way, there is only one miracle worker, our Lord Jesus Christ. Through him you can find your destination as God intended, not in faraway places but in your heart.

I know for me, if it had not been for God, my family, friends, and the Healing Place, I would have fallen off the edge. Instead, they helped me look beyond my past beliefs to a horizon whose realism exceeds my senses. Missing Kimmy has caused me to look within to the one thing I have to relate with...my soul.

Free will is the gift.

Love is the choice.

What is life to you?

A problem to be solved or a present to be opened?

Heavenly Father, like your disciples, I confess and repent with a sorrowful heart my sins. Through Christ our savior, free me, I pray, from my bondage and bless me with your mercy and love, O Lord, so with a pure heart, I may see you. Amen.

Philo Love

THE THIRD GROUP OF CHRISTIANS is free Christians. They are the followers of Christ who dwell primarily in the stage of love called *philo*.

Philo love is friendship love. It is that something you see in another person that draws you to be their friend.

A key verse for philo love comes from the book of John. While the disciples' hearts are filled with sorrow because of Jesus' impending departure, he comforts them, saying:

> *I no longer call you servants, because a servant does not know his master's business. Instead, I have called you friends, for everything I have learned from my Father I have made known to you.*
>
> —John 15:15

In calling his disciples friends, Jesus is saying that he will share with them his life and the secrets of his innermost heart. Just like it was for the disciples then, it is up to us today to accept or reject his friendship.

Unlike some people, Christ does not measure us according to the number of our wins, the esteem in which the world upholds us, or our commanding influence. On the contrary, he looks within to the very core of our being to see how far we have opened our heart. Therefore, before we can truly know the depth of Jesus' love, we must face the thought that he knows everything about each of us, sin and all.

Free Christians are followers of Christ who accept his friendship and believe that he has liberated them from the bonds of their sins. Because they are able to experience the compassion of Christ, free Christians handle suffering in a more positive way—one that allows them to mourn, offers them comfort when they do, and finally gives them hope. Besides healing, they also believe Saint Augustine's words: "God loves each of us as if there were only one of us."[18]

As free Christians and friends of Christ, the mysteries of the Kingdom of Heaven are made known. Thus, they believe "...that Christ died for our sins according to the scriptures; and that he was buried, and he rose again the third day according to his scriptures" (*I Corinthians 15:3-4*). From such a godly perspective and personal relationship with Jesus, death to free Christians is simply a doorway to his eternity.

When I was a young boy, I used to attend the North Side Youth Center. It was run by a wonderful pastor named Tru Robertson. Though kids went there to play, Tru made sure there was always some time for learning about the Bible.

The first verse I learned there was from John 3:16:

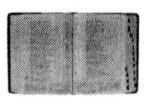

> *For God so loved the world, That he gave his only begotten son, That whosoever believeth in him should not perish, but have everlasting life.*
>
> —*John 3:16*

As a child I could recite it faultlessly. I even remember how nice I thought the words sounded. But, like a lot of other verses, its real meaning was baffling to me. Even when I became an adult, I did not completely understand what it meant. In fact, it was only recently, lost in the depths of my sorrow that I finally understood the verse's meaning. There, in the midst of my grief, the magnitude of God's grace in giving Christ to save the world crystallized in my heart. Now, even if it means going to church alone, I am drawn to the only thing that can overcome my loss…God's love.

When was the first time you recited John 3:16?

As a present day disciple, what do the Apostle John's words—"For God so loved the world"—mean to you?

Heavenly Father, I confess that I do not love you with my whole heart. Nor do I love others as I love myself. Since I've received Christ as my personal savior, teach me how to love the way you love. Break down the limitations in my heart and move me to overcome the human tendency to build walls. Lord, lead me, to reach out and embrace others as Christ embraced the cross for me. Amen.

Agape Love

THE FINAL GROUP OF CHRISTIANS is complete Christians. They dwell in the fourth stage of love called *agape*.

Agape love is godly love; a love that gives to others, not that desires for itself. Unlike eros or storge love which is never used in the New Testament, agape is mentioned over two hundred times to describe love.[19]

Many Christians are too preoccupied in showing the passion of Christ (how much Christ loved God) instead of expressing his compassion (how much God loves us). For some, revealing our Lord's compassion is too personal. Yet in a world full of loss and sorrow, we need to. Only through sharing how much God loves us so others may experience it too, are we truly obeying his commandment to love one another.

A key verse for agape love is from 1 John.

How great is the love the Father has lavished on us, that we should be called children of God! And that is what we are! The reason the world does not know us is that it

> *did not know him. Dear friends, now we are children of God, and what we will be has not yet been made known. But we know that when he appears, we shall be like him, for we shall see him as he is. Everyone who has this hope in him purifies himself, just as he is pure.*
>
> —*1 John 3:1-3*

While philo love is something that draws you to be someone's friend, agape or godly love, is a response to the grace we have received. Motivated by the love of God, our love for others becomes spontaneous and independent of our goodness.

When I was a child, I stuttered. As a consequence I grew up extremely self-conscious about speaking in public. Even after writing *Tears of Love*, I held back from speaking about our Lord's compassion. It was not until the following two events occurred, demolishing the remaining barrier around my heart that I began to speak up.

Four years after Kimmy's death, my mother learned she had cancer and had only a couple of months to live. Parked in the driveway after returning from the doctor's office, I asked her, "Mom, is there anything I can do?"

"No," she answered. "I'm not afraid of dying, but I don't want to leave my family."

"I know," I responded, looking out the window, trying to hide my tears. "But think how many will be waiting for you." And, I added, "It won't be long and we'll be with you." My mother died less than a month later.

Three months after her death, I received an early

morning phone call. It was from my sister. Our brother Darrell had died in a garage fire. Unable to speak, I handed the phone to my wife. My world was shrinking, getting smaller and smaller, and I could not stop it.

I was asked to speak at Darrell's funeral. I jotted down some notes, but nothing made any sense to me. Frustrated, I threw the notes away. There was no worldly knowledge that could make sense of what had happened—at least not in my heart. Only God held all the answers. Remembering my childhood faith, I decided to tell a story about the Apostle John, the disciple of love.

> Even when he was very old and lamed, the Apostle John continued to preach that Jesus was the Son of God and that all who believed in him would have eternal life. When visiting different churches, he always made the same request to parishioners.
>
> On one such occasion, a young man who had heard the Apostle speak before turned to a friend and said, "Listen. Before the Apostle is done, he'll say, 'Little children, love one another.' " Sure enough, he did. Later, when John was leaving the church, the young man asked him why he always beseeched us to love one another.
>
> In a feeble voice the Apostle answered, "Because that's all you need to know."

Christians who dwell in agape love are complete Christians. This does not mean they are sinless, only forgivable. Nor does it infer that they are perfect, but rather that they are actively embracing others.

Being a complete Christian is about obeying our Lord's

commandment to love one another by sharing how much God loves us.

> Do you choose to allow pain and fear to cause you to build a wall around your heart?
>
> Or will you let God's love walk you through your grief?

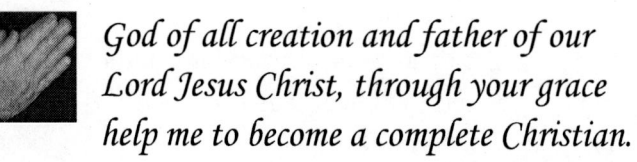

God of all creation and father of our Lord Jesus Christ, through your grace help me to become a complete Christian. Examine my heart and remove whatever sins are in my life acting as a barrier to you. Teach me, I pray, to love the way you love, so I may begin the great adventure for which you have created me. Amen.

Conclusion

AS WATER SEEKS ITS OWN LEVEL, so should we in our hearts as spiritual beings rise to the level of love that leads us to God. After helping us to understand what love is, God calls us to share it. Only by showing others how much God loves us so they may experience it also are we truly obeying his commandment to love one another.

Before I was cradled within God's light, I was plagued by the question: "Did Kimmy know how much I loved her?" After receiving God's divine light through the window, the answer came to me. I remembered my final words to her: "I love you."

I knew that was my answer and my blessing, that regardless of all my shortcomings, Kimmy *had* known how much I loved her.

Once I heard someone say, "Let your tears be like pearls for those you mourn." At the time I thought my book *Tears of Love* would be a father's last present to his daughter, a necklace of pearls. Later, as the ending became clearer, I realized that I was mistaken. Though Kimmy died at a young age, my daughter's life, like a hope chest, became a treasure chest. For sixteen years, she grew in my heart. Memories of her, like keepsakes, are still there. *Tears of Love* was a daughter's present to her father, a treasure chest of love that today shines in my heart.

The evidence of God's grace felt to me like I was given the greatest gift of all. Through *Portal of Love*, I pray it will become a blessing to you. More than a window to heaven, may it become an avenue, a way for you to continue and grow into the eternal calling that God has placed upon your life; so that in your time of need, you may know that at the end of the rainbow, the mountains do touch the sky and God is holding your hand.

I pray that out of his glorious riches, he may strengthen you with power through his spirit in your inner being, so that Christ may dwell in your heart through faith. And I pray that you being rooted and established in love, may have power, together with all the saints, to grasp how wide and long and high and deep is the love of Christ. And to know this love that surpasses knowledge—that you may be filled to the measure of all the fullness of God.
—*Ephesians 3:16-19*

PART III

A Time To Die

—Angel of Hope Memorial Garden, Eau Claire, Wisconsin

"You, O Lord, have delivered my soul from death, my eyes from tears, my feet from stumbling."
—Psalm 116:8

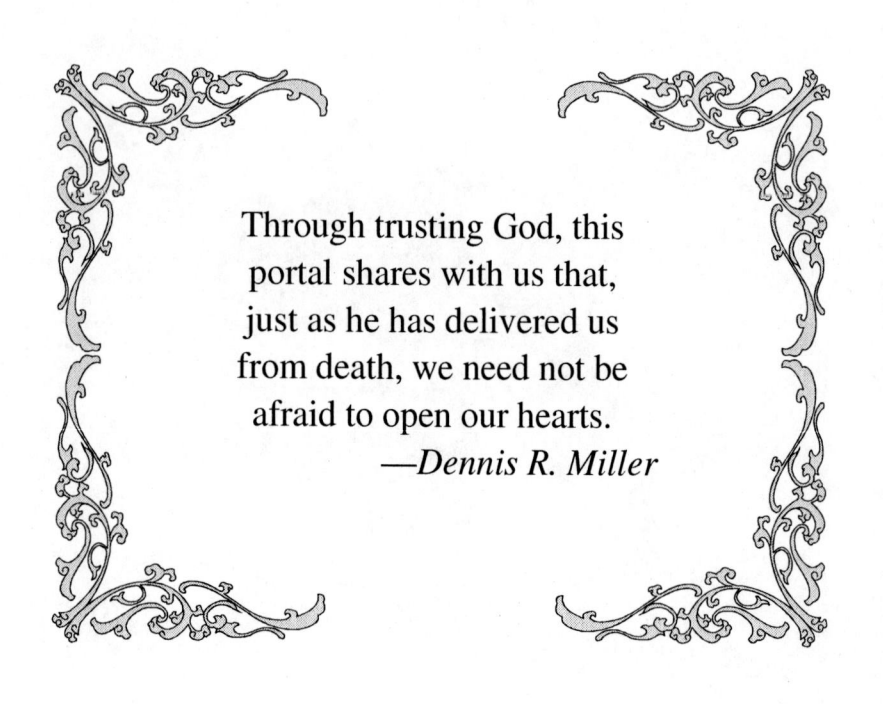

Through trusting God, this portal shares with us that, just as he has delivered us from death, we need not be afraid to open our hearts.
—*Dennis R. Miller*

A Time to Die

IN THE FAR NORTHERN HILLS OF New Hampshire lies an old and abandoned cemetery. On one of its many leaning tombstones is written:

> It is a terrible thing to love
> What death can touch.[20]

Grief is everywhere and to save ourselves, we often turn our backs on the very one that can help. Many of us abandon love like the deserted cemetery.

God's love is capable of healing hurting souls and gives us many reasons for having hope and going on. Like a breath of fresh air, we possess the medicine to soothe broken hearts.

In the beginning of my book *Tears of Love,* I wrote: "A bereaved father opens his heart to share his grief and then the only thing that overcame his loss…God's love."

Another example of God's love is Jim and Kathy Hitch. With their family of eight wonderful children, they make up the ministry Simple Grace. Together they travel the country singing and praising God.

Kathy, the lead vocal in the song, "Broken Believer," knows well how everyone at times feels pain and loss. Her broken heart came from a multitude of miscarriages. When she sings "Broken Believer," her voice resonates with deep emotion. Being a mother, she wanted to hold on tight to all the precious pieces of her heart, but as the song says, "only God holds all the pieces to your heart."[21]

Like Simple Grace, these biblical verses from Romans also show how we may honor our sisters and brothers in Christ.

> *Love must be sincere. Hate what is evil, cling to what is good. Be devoted to one another in brotherly love. Honor one another above yourself. Never be lacking in zeal, but keep your spiritual fervor serving the Lord. Be joyful in hope, patient in affliction, faithful in prayer. Share with God's people who are in need. Practice hospitality. Bless those who persecute you; bless and do not curse. Rejoice with those who rejoice; mourn with those who mourn.*
> —*Romans 12:9-15*

John Baptist Metz, a professor of fundamental theology, said, "The capacity to mourn is the measure of our humanity."[22]

When we find people who can't empathize with others, we realize that they have lost the connection between grieving and loving.

For Christians, Christ is our miracle worker. When he hung on the cross, Christ cried out:

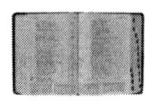

> *My God, my God, why hast thou forsaken me?*
> —*Mark 15:34*

Many suffering people today feel separated from God.

> **Can you help them bridge the gap between grieving and loving?**
>
> **Can you express to them how you found peace not in some faraway place, but in your heart?**

We do not need to be professors of theology to witness God's love. If our love is sincere and we mourn with those who mourn, then we will want to share our compassion with God's people who are also in need.

For many of us, it is difficult to witness to others; but God has provided a way that we can overcome our inhibitions. There are two truths everyone can agree to: that we are all born and that we will all die. As we progress in our life from birth to death, God did not intend for us to be overcome by worry, anxiety, and burdens. On the contrary, instead of quenching our spirits with worry and fear, God wants us to trust in him.

Recently, filmmaker Dean Bauman experienced firsthand our need to confide in and rely on God. On the evening of May 31, 2006, I was at Dean's studio, working on the *Window to Heaven* DVD with him. During a break, Dean handed me a poem he had written several years earlier that was inspired from Ecclesiastes 3:12 and John 5:24-30.

"Please tell me what you think of it," Dean asked.

A Time to Die

Someone you love has just passed away;
Maybe very young, or a long-lived age.
You want to believe this is somehow a bad dream;
You're crying, losing sleep, and maybe saying;
"Why has this happened to me?"
You've laid them down to rest,
left now to wonder and think;
You're searching your heart through,
Trying to find the missing link.
Maybe you feel that you have
taken their life for granted;
But the good memories you've shared
are inside your heart planted.
Remember their smile and the
wonderful moments you've shared;
They are now in God's hand,
and await to see you there.
Now is the time to search deep within your heart;
Live after death through Jesus,
You will never ever be apart.
God promises us through Christ,
You shall see them again in time;

For the answers are there to find.
Remember what you can about Jesus, our Christ;
He opened the door to the grave,
but He had to pay a price.
If who you have lost was a Brother, Sister,
A Husband, a Wife, a Child, or a Friend;
Do not be troubled, dear soul,
you can see them in heaven again.
Jesus wants you to know Him,
so you can be comforted and secure;
Heaven is a better place for them,
so please, let go of your fears.
They only left before you
so they could greet you from on High;
God will comfort your tears and your sorrows,
But there shall always be,
A Time to Die.[23]

—*Dean Bauman*

After reading the poem, I turned to Dean and told him that it was well written and very relevant to the video we were producing.

"Thank you," Dean said. "You know what's odd? I've never lost anyone close to me. Strange, huh?"

"You're lucky," I answered. "No matter who we are, if we live long enough, we will all feel the touch of death."

Dean nodded his head yes.

Still, neither of us was prepared for what happened next.

The following morning Dean called me. "You were right. Like a thief, death has robbed me. My brother committed suicide last night."

Dean was older than his brother, yet the two of them were regularly mistaken for twins. Besides looking alike, they were best friends.

"Why did this happen the day after I shared my poem with you?" Then he answered himself, "Why not?"

Words could not express the pain I felt for Dean. His loss and pain reminded me of an elderly gentleman I met after a presentation who wanted me to autograph my book *Tears of Love* for him.

As I was signing the book, he asked, "Don't they know what they do? My son," he explained, "committed suicide a few years ago. I never knew grief until then. I felt so guilty because I wasn't there for him."

Rather bitterly he said, "Of course there were the know-it-alls who felt obliged to tell me that my son wouldn't go to heaven because he took his own life."

After taking a long breath, he asked me, "Why did he do it? Didn't he know what it would do to his loved ones, to me?"

"No, I don't believe he did," I answered, "and you can't blame yourself." I put my hand on his shoulder. "Only God knows who will or will not go to heaven."

"Thank you." He squeezed my hand, "I needed to hear that."

While many who are grief-stricken will sweep the pain into some dark corner of their heart, Dean did not do that. Instead, as his brother's keeper, his love led to an awakening of his heart that turned his focus outward, away from himself to others. From his sorrow, Dean produced a video of the memorable parable that Jesus used to describe God's everlasting love for us—*The Prodigal Son*.

Since none of us know when we will take our last breath, let us rejoice and stand in awe today, amazed at all God's done. Now is the time when dreams can come true.

Like the disciple Peter sought to come to Christ by walking on water, singer Dawn Cripe, who by the grace of God has overcome the wounds of an abusive past, wrote and recorded the CD "Rescued and Restored." In song seven, "I Wanna Run," Dawn steps out in faith to reveal her hope that "Christ is who she's been dreaming of."[24]

If we don't take a chance and dance, life can pass us by. As I said to Dean, we will all feel the touch of death, either from losing those we love or, eventually, our own passing.

As Christians, we should not be afraid of death. Just as Jesus told the story of the prodigal son to express God's love, he continues to enlighten us today. Our heavenly Father eagerly awaits to embrace and welcome us and helps us to deal with our fears.

According to Bill Gaultiere, Ph.D., "there are more than 365 'fear nots' in the Bible!"[25]

> **So why are so many Christians afraid of death?**
>
> **Is it a matter of heart?**

I believe that the longest eighteen inches can be that between our head and heart. Too often we think about God's love rather than marvel at its wonderfulness.

In 1994 Henri Nouwen wrote the *Return of the Prodigal Son*. In this story of homecoming, he said:

> He left the house of his heavenly Father, came to a foreign country, gave away all that he had, and returned through a cross to his Father's home. All of this he did, not as a rebellious son, but as the obedient son, sent out to bring home all the lost children of God...Jesus is the prodigal son of the prodigal Father who gave away everything the Father had entrusted to him so that I could become like him and return with him to his Father's house.[26]

Like the prodigal son, God wants everyone bound in sorrow and grief to seek the fullness of him. In part two, we stated that "Free will is the gift, love is the choice." If we choose love, no matter what bars surround us, our faith can set us free.

In this world where death and loss come all too often, Christ can comfort us. Jesus said:

> *I am the living one who died. Look, I am alive forever and ever! And I hold the keys of death and the grave.*
> —*Revelation 1:18*

Many people frequently turn away from those who are experiencing the actual emotions behind their grief. Often terminal patients lie in hospital rooms waiting to die while the people they love come and go as visitors.

John, an elderly man, was dying from lung cancer. He

was sent to the hospital because his parents had long ago passed away, his wife wasn't physically up to taking care of him, and his children were too busy.

An old veteran, John was not afraid of dying. During the Korean War, he had faced death often, alongside many fallen comrades. What bothered him now was dying alone.

One morning before dawn, the male night nurse peeked into John's room. Noting that he was awake, the nurse asked if there was anything he would like.

The grizzled veteran shook his head no; but then, when the nurse turned to leave, John spoke. Just as his body lay in a near fetal position, his mind had regressed to when he was a sick child. He described how warm and secure he felt cuddled in his mother's arms.

The old veteran coughed and gasped for breath. In the end John, who was just a skeleton compared to his former self, died in the nurse's arms. Tears rolled down the nurse's cheeks, tears of love for John and tears of sorrow for his own father who had recently passed away.

Has your life been affected by the death of someone you loved?

What was your response?

When Kimmy died, it broke my heart.

Years later, sitting by my mother's side when she passed away, I was surprised, at my age, by how lost I felt.

Three months after her death, we received a phone call

telling us that my brother had died in a garage fire, I had to hand the phone to my wife. I couldn't talk.

Death is life's ultimate reality check. We are here not to fill a space but because we need to be filled and come to terms with our own mortality. In his gospel John the disciple tells how Christ promised him that the Holy Spirit would come and help them. The promise is the same for us today.

> *But the counselor, the Holy Spirit, whom the Father will send in my name will teach you all things and will remind you of everything I have said to you. Peace I leave with you; my peace I give you. I do not give to you as the world gives. Do not let your hearts be troubled and do not be afraid.*
>
> —*John 14:26-27*

As a child I used to love family reunions, especially all the delicious food. With the appetite of a growing boy, I'd eat until I was stuffed and couldn't eat anymore. By the next day, however, I'd be hungry and think of the family reunion and all the food I didn't eat.

Today, when I remember those family reunions of my youth, it is not the food I miss but the people. When I think of them, my heart often swells with regret for the things I did not do. Little things, like visiting them more often. Perhaps that is the way with most of us. We need to grow up before we know what matters most.

When I hear today about how many of us fear death, I

am reminded what someone once told me: Our concept of heaven determines our acceptance of death. As a Christian, I imagine heaven like a homecoming. What a joyful banquet it will be. A continuous family reunion with God at its head and me surrounded by all the loved ones I have known.

Conclusion

MAY GOD'S LOVE EMPOWER THE Holy Spirit to seek and comfort the hearts of all broken believers. Just as Jesus came from the heart of God to reveal his love, God wants to place his love in our hearts. Don't let fear distract you from the will of God. The Vine dictionary states that "love can be known only from the action it prompts."[27] As human beings our capacity to mourn is a measure of our spirituality or how much we have become like Christ. God will not forsake us nor give us more than we can handle. Rather, like an earthly father would take his worn and tired children up to bed, we may trust that he will carry us.

Just like the following message the Apostle Paul wrote to the church in Rome nearly 2000 years ago was true then, its authenticity is the same for us now.

> *Who shall separate us from the love of Christ? Shall trouble or hardship or persecution or famine or nakedness or danger or sword? As it is written: "For your sake we face death all day long; we are considered as sheep to be slaughtered." No, in all these things we*

are more than conquerors through him who loved us. For I am convinced that neither death nor life, neither angels nor demons, neither the present nor the future nor any powers, neither height nor depth, nor anything else in all creation, will be able to separate us from the love of God that is in Christ Jesus our Lord.

—Romans 8:35-39

PART IV

Born Again

—Angel of Hope Memorial Garden, Eau Claire, Wisconsin

*"Show me your ways, O Lord, teach me your paths;
guide me in your truth and teach me, for you are my God,
my Savior, and my hope is in you all day long."*
—Psalm 25:4-5

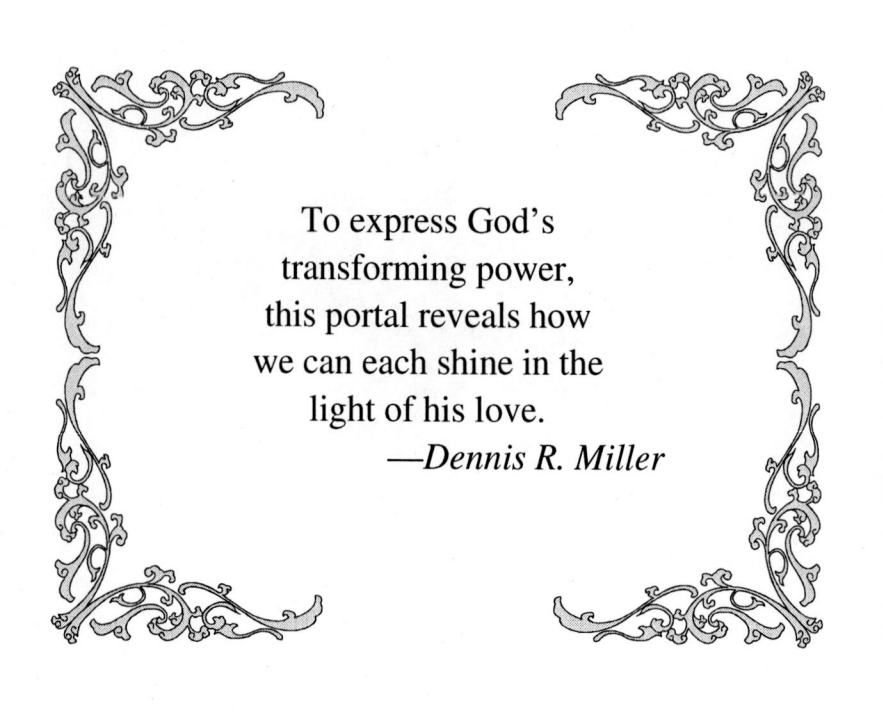

To express God's
transforming power,
this portal reveals how
we can each shine in the
light of his love.
—*Dennis R. Miller*

Born Again

When I was a child, I observed two groups of people: the young and the old. Then, because those in the old group seemed like the only ones to die, I was glad that I was in the young group. Today, like you, I know better.

> **Though there will always be a time to die, do you believe we can be reborn?**

In John 3:4-7, Nicodemus asked: "How can a man be born when he is old? Surely he cannot enter a second time into his mother's womb to be born!"

Jesus answered, "I tell you the truth, no one can enter the kingdom of God unless he is born of water and the spirit. Flesh gives birth to flesh, but the spirit gives birth to spirit. You should not be surprised at my saying, you must be born again."

> **What does it mean to be born again?**

It means that you have received God's spirit, life, and presence into your heart by accepting the Lord Jesus Christ as your Savior from sin, death, and judgment.

As water seeks its own level, so should we in our heart—as spiritual beings—rise to the level of love that leads us to God.

Just as I learned after the death of my daughter Kimmy that my love for her would never die, through this final portal of love, I saw how the love that caused Christ to die for us is the same love that sent the Holy Spirit to guide us today. *Born Again* is a reminder of this love and the communion of God's Holy Spirit through the life changing powers of our resurrected Savior.

> **As a spiritual being have you risen to the level of love that leads you to God?**

This portal takes us to various realities of the human condition and shows how God's transforming love liberates us to become what we were created for.

Dear Friends, let us love one another for love comes from God. Everyone

> *who loves has been born of God and knows God. Whoever does not love does not know God because God is love. This is how God showed his love among us: He sent his one and only son into the world that we might live through him. This is love; not that we loved God but that he loved us and sent his son as an atoning sacrifice for our sins.*
>
> *Dear Friends, since God so loved us, we also ought to love one another. No one has ever seen God, but if we love one another, God lives in us and his love is made complete in us.*
>
> —1 John 4:7-12

Often a bereaved Christian can falter because of his or her grief and feel lost from God's love. Even today, as much as I have talked and written about grief, there are moments when missing my daughter Kimmy overcomes me. Inside one of these pockets of grief, I was comforted by an article written in the *Compassionate Friends Newsletter* by Mary Lingle.

> We quickly find there are no words to describe the experience of losing a child. For those who have not lost a child, no explanation will do. For those who have, no explanation is necessary.[28]

Besides re-inspiring me, the article reminded me of the Apostle Paul's words regarding the spirit.

> *In the same way the spirit helps us in our weakness. We do not know what we ought to pray for, but the spirit himself intercedes for us with groans that words cannot express.*
>
> —Romans 8:25

For Christians, the Holy Spirit is much more than a moderator. He heals our soul by renewing our spirit. Throughout his ministry on earth, Jesus taught reconciliation between us and God. Often he referred to *a time is coming* when we would become redeemably restored to God. Jesus pointed out to a Samaritan woman that where we worship is not as important as the attitude of the worshiper.

> *Jesus declared, "Believe me, woman, a time is coming when you will worship the Father neither on this mountain nor in Jerusalem. You Samaritans worship what you do not know; we worship what we do know, for salvation is from the Jews. Yet a time is coming and has now come when the true worshipers will worship the father in spirit and truth, for they are the kind of worshipers the Father seeks. God is spirit, and his worshipers must worship in spirit and truth."*
>
> —John 4:21-24

While it was of paramount significance that Jesus came into the world, it was just as consequential when he went away. Jesus explained to his disciples why he must go.

Before Jesus went back to the Father, he could only heal physically sick people, but now because Christ is in us in the person of his Holy Spirit, he can heal broken souls. The time Jesus promised us has come. The spirit we had lost because of Adam's sin has been rekindled within us. In death Christ became our miracle worker, the way between God and us, our connection between grieving and loving.

God has provided those in the desert of suffering an avenue of deliverance. According to the prophet Isaiah, God was already preparing a way for his people before Christ was born.

And a highway will be there;
it will be called the way of Holiness.
The unclean will not journey on it;
it will be for those who walk in that way;
wicked fools will not go about on it.
No lion will be there,
nor will any ferocious beast get upon it;
they will not be found there.
But only the redeemed will walk there,
and the ransomed of the Lord will return.
They will enter Zion with singing;
everlasting joy will crown their heads.

*Gladness and joy will overtake them,
and sorrow and sighing will flee away.*
            —*Isaiah 35:8-10*

> **Do you know how the Holy Spirit can help you to continue on?**

In Eau Claire, Wisconsin, adjacent to Lakeview Cemetery, is the Angel of Hope Memorial Garden. Each year on December 6 at 7 P.M., parents, relatives, and friends come together at the garden. There, during a candlelight service, they pay homage to their children. The ceremony is simple. A member of the Angel of Hope Association will pass on any pertinent news. Then he or she will recite something appropriate, usually a poem. After that, one by one, the families come forth carrying a candle. In front of the Angel of Hope statue, they turn to face the others and say their child's name and perhaps something they cherish about their loved one. When all have come forth, they conclude the candle light vigil by singing "Silent Night" together.

Though it is usually very cold and some are quick to leave after the song is over, there are always those who linger. It is then that the words on the plaque at the garden's entrance resonate the most.

> Our hope, we are reminded from the angel's
> outstretched arms, is that someday our mourning will

become less about grieving, and more about loving. Loving a loved one who has passed on, loving yourself to go on with your life, and finally, loving life to accept its eternal gift that this love lives forever.

Until then, may we all find shelter within these praying hands and comfort in the truth, that of all the virtues, love is the greatest.

Even though *enough* is a difficult word to measure something by, for all who are lost and mourning, I wish you *enough* that *your sorrow and sighing flee away.*

It wasn't because of a lack of knowledge that Nicodemus failed to understand what Christ meant by being born again. As a Jewish teacher and a member of a group of religious leaders called Pharisees, he knew the Old Testament thoroughly. On the contrary, it was the lack of spiritual fulfillment that caused him not to perceive what Christ said.

According to the American Religious Identification Survey 2008, only 34 percent of American adults claim that they have been reborn.[29] We need a spiritual awakening. We, the church, have to get out of the maintenance mode that we are stuck in and start reaching out.

Like the early disciples before Jesus ascended to heaven, many of us today believe he is the Messiah but fail to understand the true significance of his death and resurrection. During the preparation of his last supper, Jesus knew that the disciples were unable to grasp all that he told them. Thus, after washing their feet, he sought to reassure them and said:

> *I have told you this, so that when the time comes you will remember that I warned you. I did not tell you this at first because I was with you.*
>
> *Now I am going to him who sent me, yet none of you ask me, where are you going? Because I have said these things, you are filled with grief. But I tell you the truth: It is for your good that I am going away. Unless I go away, the counselor will not come to you; but if I go, I will send him to you.*
>
> —John 16:4-7

After the cross and his resurrection, the disciples found out what Jesus had referred to—"for your good." As Saint Augustine describes: "You ascended from before our eyes. We turned back grieving, only to find you in our hearts."[30]

Does Christ dwell within you today?

Besides recognizing him as your Lord and Savior through the presence of his Holy Spirit, have you welcomed him into your heart?

To have our life in God and not in things, circumstances, or ourselves, we need to be filled with the

Holy Spirit. Thankfully, the love of God in Christ Jesus as revealed to us through the Bible is full of spiritual instructions. Just as Jesus healed the blind men in Matthew 9:27-30 by telling them, "According to your faith will it be done to you," so he will heal our spiritual blindness today according to our faith. While personal holiness is a work of gradual development and not a onetime event, through God's grace we can move forward, one step at a time.

There are five spiritual guidelines the Bible uses to show us the way.

1. Self-Examination
2. Confession of all Known Sin
3. Yield Ourselves unto God
4. Ask God to be Filled with his Holy Spirit
5. Give Thanks

STEP I

Self-Examination

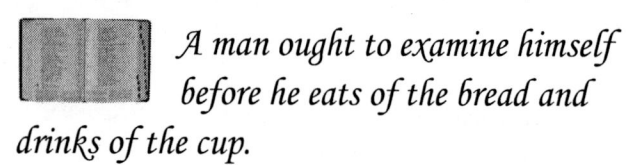

> *A man ought to examine himself before he eats of the bread and drinks of the cup.*
>
> —*1 Corinthians 11:28*

UNLESS WE EXAMINE OURSELVES through healthy introspection, we will become like the Israelites and wander the desert of despair and bitterness. Christians seeking to be filled with the Holy Spirit should regularly examine themselves to see if they are continuously glorifying Jesus.

In my early Christian life, I felt uncomfortable going to church alone. After Karen and I lost Kimmy, my perspective began to change. I joined a small Bible study group at church, started to sing in our church choir and began volunteering to do odd jobs around our church.

When the custodian planned to go on vacation for a week, I offered to take his place. The experience was very uplifting for me. First, I saw that a church isn't only a one hour event, one day per week. The church hums like a beehive every day. Members are busy taking care of children, sewing quilts for world relief, preparing local meals, studying in Bible classes, organizing mission teams, and more. They make the intangible become touchable and alive.

The richest reward I received for my service happened when I cleaned the sanctuary. As I went along the pews, picking up pieces of paper, crayons, and pencils, I noticed a little plastic baggy of Cheerios. I picked it up and smiled to myself, remembering when our children were little.

After I was through mopping around the altar, I turned to sit on the steps and take a break. Facing the sanctuary from the altar, I was overcome with a sense of unity and recognized how much each of us is part of the greater whole—part of God's family.

For many Christians, it is difficult to worship God in spirit. For most of my life, I was this way. While I could easily relate to God the Father and God the Son, I couldn't grasp God the Holy Spirit. No other feeling, however, causes us to re-examine our life more than grief. After Kimmy's death, I felt lost and deeply in need of something more. Such a need moves us into a contemplative state and helps us to look within ourselves for the deeper meaning and purpose of life.

For you who are grieving:

> May the God who gives endurance and encouragement give you a spirit of unity among yourselves as you follow Christ Jesus, so that with one heart and mouth you may glorify the God and Father of our Lord Jesus Christ.

STEP II

Confession of all Known Sin

> *If we confess our sins, he is faithful and just to forgive us our sins, and to cleanse us from all unrighteousness.*
>
> —*1 John 1:9*

WHEN A LIGHT IS BROUGHT INTO A ROOM, what was a window becomes also a mirror, reflecting back images of what lies within. Because the Holy Spirit enters only into clean vessels, after we examine ourselves, we should confess all sin brought to mind. We need to cleanse our hearts of idle hope, of earthly desires and flattery. When we see the uselessness of temporal greatness, we are observing the awakening signs of God's spirit working in us. Then we are beginning, as Henry Nouwen said: "To set your affections on things above, not on things of the earth."[31]

Repenting means to acknowledge the truth in our Lord's Gospels and turning away from our old ways, yet no one is capable of bringing a clean thing out of an unclean thing but God. Therefore, like David, we need to ask God to cleanse us from within.

> *Create in me a pure heart, O God, and renew a steadfast spirit within me. Do not cast me from your presence or take your Holy Spirit from me. Restore to me the joy of your salvation and grant me a willing spirit, to sustain me.*
>
> —*Psalms 51:10-12*

STEP III
Yield Ourselves unto God

Likewise reckon ye also yourselves to be dead indeed unto sin, but alive unto God through Jesus Christ our Lord.

Let not sin therefore reign in your mortal body, that ye should obey it in the lusts thereof.

Neither yield ye your members as instruments of unrighteousness unto sin; but yield yourselves unto God, as those that are alive from the dead, and your members as instruments of righteousness unto God.

—*Romans 6:11-13 (King James Version)*[32]

TO BE FILLED WITH HIS SPIRIT, we must yield ourselves to his spirit. God's love seeks to move us to overcome the human tendency to build walls and leads us to reach out and embrace others. Yet, according to Henry Newman, "So much holiness is lost to the church because men refuse to share the secrets of their hearts with one another."[33]

In Luke 5:4, Jesus told Simon, Peter, and the other

fisherman in the boat with him: "Put out into the deep..., and lower your nets for a haul."

> **As a Christ follower today, do you want to haul in the blessings of God's love in your life?**

If yes, then like the disciples of old, we too must leave the comfortable and shallow way of living and seek the deeper water. To yield ourselves unto God, we must thus trust and submit our hearts completely to him.

For someone who is just beginning their spiritual journey by stepping out in faith, God reveals himself to us in many ways. For instance, those awe-inspiring moments when the world of the spiritual and the world of the physical meet, or by some unusual timing or linkage. By this last means, God answered a question that had plagued me.

It began when my wife Karen decided to write the orphanage in Korea where Kimmy had come from. She wanted to inform them that Kimmy had died. Not having the address, she went to Lutheran Social Services (LSS), the agency we adopted our daughter through.

After listening to Karen, the director at LSS was so taken in by her sincerity that she asked if we would like to adopt a child from the Philippines. At the time Karen said no. "We're too old," she explained. "Think about it anyway," the director said.

When Karen told me what had been proposed, I agreed

with my wife. It was a nice gesture but we were too old. Later, however, when our son David was about to graduate from high school, we had a change of heart.

During David's graduation party, we informed family and friends that we had decided to adopt an older child from the Philippines. Though most were happy for us, there were a few skeptics who thought we were trying to replace Kimmy.

I knew better. I had cried too much over the loss of Kimmy. My heart was more than acutely aware there will only be one of her. Still, when I tried to explain why we had decided to adopt again, my attempts to answer those who questioned our motives fell short.

One of the conditions for adoption in the Philippines is that you must spend a week there to become familiar with your child's culture and to learn what he or she has been through. Midway through our week, the answer for adopting again came to me.

We had spent a long day traveling the outskirts of Manila. When we finally returned to the hotel, I suggested that we take a break in the lounge. To my surprise, the moment we sat down a woman who was singing there asked me unexpectedly if I had a request. I could not think of the name of any song; but I vaguely remembered one I liked from a movie. I replied, "What about the song in *Titanic*." "A beautiful one," she said and smiled.

The singer had a wonderful voice. When she began to sing the song, it made me want to dance. Though I love to dance, I am shy and prefer not to be the first or only one on the floor. I waited for someone else to get up, but nobody did. Feeling that it would be a terrible waste not to fully enjoy the music, I got up and asked Karen to dance. We were the only Caucasians there. Everyone else was either from China, Japan, or the Philippines.

When the song ended and Karen and I started to leave the floor to sit down, everyone in the lounge clapped. It was at that instant that the answer came to me. It was in the name of the song, "My Heart Will Go On."

Instead of trying to see what you can do, have you yielded yourself to God to see what he will do?

STEP IV

Ask God to be Filled with his Holy Spirit

> *If ye, then, being evil, know how to give good gifts unto your children, how much more shall your heavenly Father give the Holy Spirit to them that ask him?*
>
> —*Luke 11:13*

THE FOURTH INSTRUCTION THE BIBLE offers us is probably the simplest of the five spiritual instructions. It is not always easy to ask God to fill us with his Holy Spirit. There was a woman who was having great difficulty in grieving the death of her husband. After a year had lapsed, she decided to go for help. Through counseling and much self-examination, she learned that the breakdown between her grieving and loving was over something that had occurred a long time ago. She was still angry with her father though he had died many years earlier. The more she indulged in selfishness and allowed her anger to dominate her emotions, the worse she grieved over the passing of her husband. In other words, her heart could not go on and heal from the death of her husband until she stopped hating her father.

Just as fear stifles the spirit within us, so anger can restrain us from asking to be filled with the Holy Spirit. Before this woman could open her heart, she had to confess her anger and submit it to God.

STEP V

Give Thanks

In everything give thanks: for this is the will of God in Christ Jesus concerning you.

—*1 Thessalonians 5:18*

THIS IS THE FINAL BIBLICAL INSTRUCTION that guides us to the way of holiness.

> **But, for any of us who have lost a loved one, how can we ever again be thankful?**

This question places me in front of my daughter Kimmy's casket again. I remember holding her girlfriend's baby and wishing it was Kimmy just arriving from Korea. I am reminded of the Native Americans and the difficulty they had in understanding how anyone could own the land. Like the water and the sky, they believed it belonged to the Great Spirit too. While handing the baby back to her mother, I thought, *Children belong to God also, and we can only hold them for a moment.*

So how can we be thankful again?

While it does seem like only a moment that we have held our loved ones in our arms, we will forever hold them in our hearts and souls. And when we depart from this place of time to witness up close the glory of God, we shall reflect his image and see that our loved ones have always been a part of us.

When I was born, there were some family members who told my mother to place me in an orphanage. She would not hear of it. One of her enduring expressions I fondly remember is her always calling me—"my son."

Sitting by her side when she died from cancer at age 87, I was surprised at how much I felt like an orphan.

An hour later the funeral director asked us if we'd like to view her remains once more before he took them away. I became upset. *How could he refer to her as remains?*

Through God's grace I wasn't angry long. Instead, I was reminded how Jesus promised us the Holy Spirit.

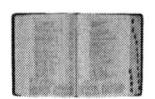

> *"I will not leave you as orphans; I will come to you."*
>
> —John 14:18

Conclusion

THE SPIRIT OF TRUTH GIVES US a whole new perspective on life. Now I know that the funeral director was correct. What he took away was my mother's earthly remains. But just as I reminded my mother about her loved ones waiting to be reunited with her, I know that she is anticipating my homecoming.

> **Through his Holy Spirit has Christ come to you?**

By faith, I believe that God often touches us through people. By my faith in his word, I am sure Kimmy is okay. And by my faith in his promises, my heart has gone on. Today it is with a grateful heart that I thank God for all the wonderful moments he has allowed me to share in his love; through my wife Karen to whom I dedicated this book to, my sons Patrick, Erin, and David, and the sixteen precious years with Kimmy. God has richly blessed me. Moreover, today, I thank him for the little girl from the Philippines who is a woman now, our lovely daughter Michelle. What a joy it has been to watch her grow and become who she is.

Life with all its ups and downs forms us into diamonds with each one of our facets representing someone we love. My hope for everyone is that we all love one another and thus become like the meaning of Michelle's name—Who is like God.

Just like a caterpillar is created to be transformed into a butterfly, we were formed to become born again and to spiritually evolve into the image of Christ. I hope this portal has encouraged you to step out in faith and become what you were created for.

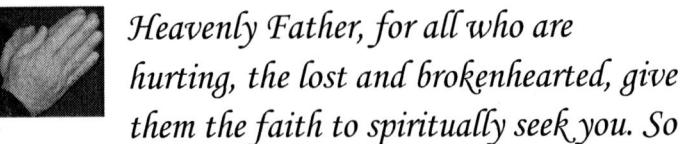

Heavenly Father, for all who are hurting, the lost and brokenhearted, give them the faith to spiritually seek you. So their heart may go on, let them see that love doesn't die. Show them that just as your eminence is present throughout the entire universe by your Holy Spirit, so is the presence of our loved ones. That their spirit abides in the heavenly places wherein our soul dwells, where the unseen world of spiritual reality exists. As born again believers, we thank Christ for the precious moments when glorifying him has become the joy of our life. Hear us now as we praise you for being a great and wonderful God. Amen.

Postlude

IT IS EASY TO MISS A PARTICULAR TREE in a forest; it is also easy to miss something that should be there but is not. As a member of the YMCA, I try to do the walking track three times a week. I have noticed banners from various organizations hanging around the track saying that they care about our community, only the names are different.

On the wall near the entrance to the YMCA is a large plaque. Written in bold brass letters within its oak frame is the following verse:

> Whatever you do,
> work at it with all your heart,
> as though you were working
> for the Lord and not for man.
> —Col. 3-23

In response to the above verse, I wish there was one banner at the YMCA that said: GOD CARES because throughout our community there are people who question if God cares.

Yesterday, it was a boy who didn't know his father. He

wonders...*Where is God?*

Today, a homeless woman with two young children will ask...*Does God care?*

Tomorrow, a bereaved mother will receive a sympathy card that says: "The Lord gives and the Lord takes, blessed be the name of the Lord." *How can I thank God?* she will ask. *His son rose from the dead, my child did not. God doesn't care.*

At the time the bereaved mother told me about the sympathy card she had received, I had no answer for her query. I could only hope that through tears, time, and reflection, she would stop blaming God for her loss. Today, through *Portals of Love*, we can see that God is not the cause of our pain but the love that guides us through it.

Out of love, God seeks to restore us. Just like being born again, healing from loss God's way is a day-by-day experience in faith until one day you will feel like the very air in a bubble about to burst. I know he can shape our hearts to that fullness of life for which we long.

As a father who once stood over his child's grave and questioned how I could still be alive when it felt like my heart was buried, I know God cares. His love was the only thing that helped me overcame my loss. Like visions of grace, I hope and pray that *Portals of Love* has shown how much God loves you.

Heavenly Father, thank you for your unfailing grace. When we are confused, lost and brokenhearted, it guides and makes a way for us where none seems to be.

Through our faith in you, may we evermore observe your windows of grace as portals of love, ways for us to continue and shine in the light of your love. Amen

Epilogue

ONE SPRING EVENING YEARS AGO while taking the garbage out to the road, I paused to remember where Kimmy's trampoline used to be set up in our front yard. Though there was a beautiful star-filled sky above me, I felt only despair. The vacant spot where the trampoline used to be, like the sadness in my heart, made me feel that I was standing at the edge of the earth looking up and wondering, *Is there anything beyond?*

In the beginning I mention that going to the grief support center taught me how everyone who is grieving needs to tell their story. Another thing I was told was that we would survive for three reasons: because we do not have a choice; for the sake of our other loved ones; and, then, for some good we may do. When I was lost in grief, the third explanation, *for what good I could do*, went completely over my head. Being loved is the most powerful motivation there is. For me, it was not until after God's love started to crystallize in my heart, that I began to understand the third reason.

The good we may do does not need to be an impossible task. Rather it can be simple things like making a garden. Today, thanks to the Lord, there is no vacant spot in my front yard. Instead, there is a sunken Oriental garden in its place. At night I often stroll the outer circumference lit by soft lighting, before stepping down into the center. For me, the outward track has became a spiritual path similar to walking a labyrinth.

A great loss makes us question our own mortality and our very place in the world. Whatever your beliefs may be, as you traverse *the stepping stones*, mourning is challenging. And yet, another day will come, when your heart is no longer broken, when you will become the light that shines away the darkness of another's grief. Yes, then you will sit in a garden and dwell in God's blessing of hope and joy. Within his peace you will ponder like St. Francis of Assisi did, over the good you may do.

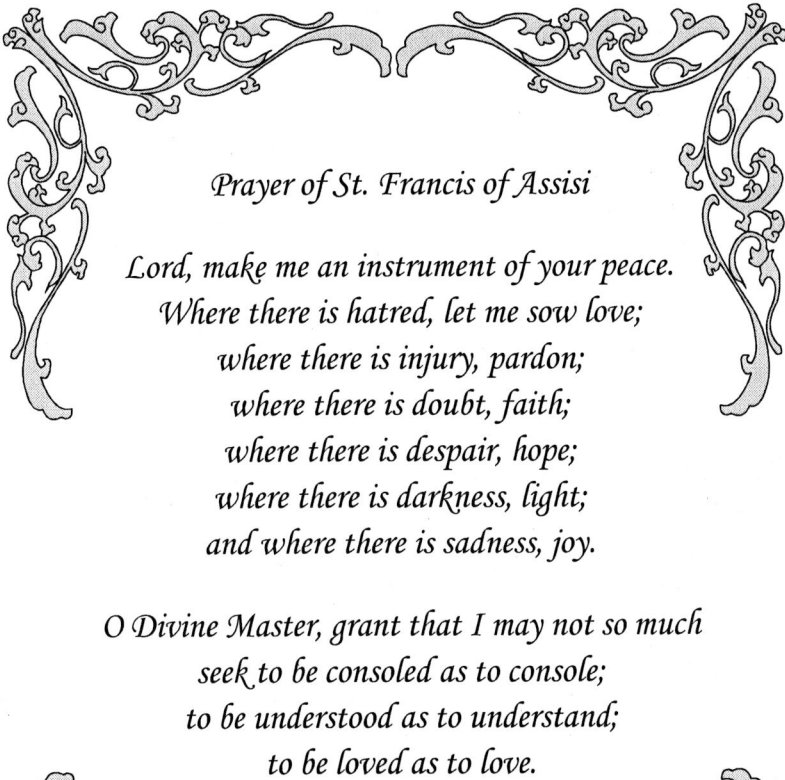

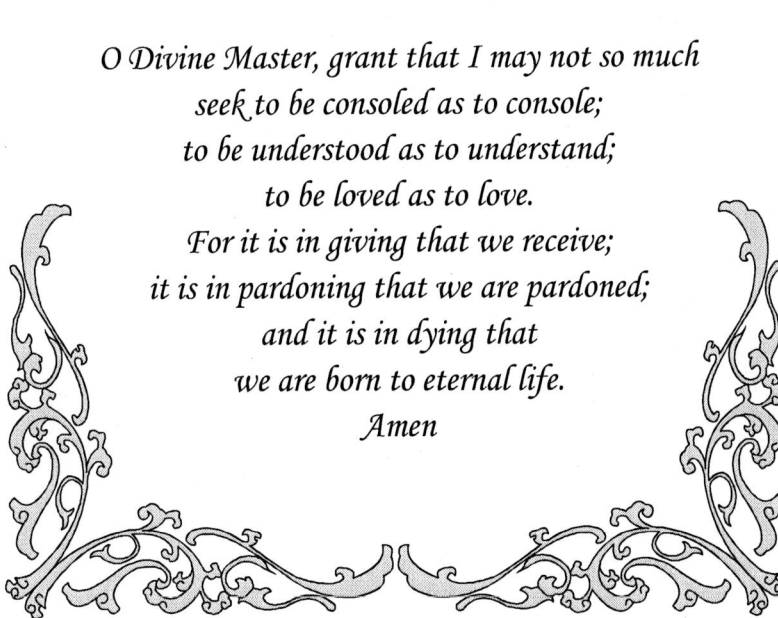

Prayer of St. Francis of Assisi

Lord, make me an instrument of your peace.
Where there is hatred, let me sow love;
where there is injury, pardon;
where there is doubt, faith;
where there is despair, hope;
where there is darkness, light;
and where there is sadness, joy.

O Divine Master, grant that I may not so much
seek to be consoled as to console;
to be understood as to understand;
to be loved as to love.
For it is in giving that we receive;
it is in pardoning that we are pardoned;
and it is in dying that
we are born to eternal life.
Amen

Notes

[1] Hunt, William. *Guidelines for Helping People*. Tampa: Christian Helplines, 2000. [p. iv]
[2] Davidson, Glen. Excerpts from talks as quoted in "Grief and Mourning." BabyNet. Accessed 13 Feb 2010, <http://www.babynetky.com/grief.html>. [p. iv]
[3] Bertolon Center for Grief & Healing. *Myths and Facts About Grief*. Hospice of the North Shore. Accessed 30 July 2010, <http://www.hns.org/Bertolon_Center_for_Grief_Healing/The_Grieving_Process.aspx>. [p. v]
[4] Kubler-Ross, Elisabeth, M.D. *Real Taste of Life: A Journal*. Durango: Viesti: Collection, 2002. [p. v]
[5] W., Bill. *Twelve Steps and Twelve Traditions*. New York: The A.A. Grapevine, Inc. and Alcoholics Anonymous Publishing, 1981. [p. vi]
[6] Stephens, Simon, Rev. "Hope." Quoted in *The Compassionate Friends: Seattle King County Chapter* Newsletter, Nov-Dec 2009. Accessed 22 Aug 2010, <http://www.tcfseattle.org/news/NovemberDecember2009.pdf>. [p. vii]
[7] Warren, Rick. *The Purpose Driven Life*. Grand Rapids, Michigan: Zondervan, 2002. [p. 2]
[8] Stephens, Simon, Rev. Quoted in *The Compassionate Friends Lehigh Valley Chapter* Mission Statement, © 2008. Accessed 12 Aug 2010, <http://www.lehighvalleytcf.org>. [p. 6]
[9] Kubler-Ross, Elisabeth, M.D. *On Death and Dying*. New York: The Macmillan Company, 1969. [p. 13]
[10] Davidson, Glen. [p. 19]
[11] FamilyDoctor.org editorial staff. "Grieving: Facing Illness, Death and Other Losses." FamilyDoctor.org, 2009. Accessed 10 Aug 2010, <http://familydoctor.org/online/famdocen/home/articles/079.html>. [p. 19]
[12] Jampolsky, Gerald, M.D. Quoted by Pastor William E. Hippin in "Chaplain's Corner." *DKPD Newsletter*, 1.22 (2008). Accessed 12 Aug 2010, <http://web.co.dekalb.ga.us/DK_Police/pdf/dkpdnewsletter090208.pdf>. [p. 22]
[13] Langer, Gary. *Analysis*. ABCNEWS/Beliefnet poll. Accessed 13 Feb 2010, <http://abcnews.go.com/sections/us/DailyNews/beliefnet_poll_010718.html>. [p. 29]

[14] Saint Augustine. Quoted by The Radical Academy in "The Philosophy of St. Augustine." © 1998-99, 2000-01, 2002-03 by The Radical Academy. Accessed 07 July 2010, <http://www.radicalacademy.com/philaugustine1.htm>. [p. 29]

[15] Peck, M. Scott. *Further Along the Road Less Traveled.* New York: Simon & Schuster, 1978. [p. 34]

[16] BrainyQuote. "Helen Keller Quotes." © 2010 by BrainyMedia.com. Accessed 24 July 2010, <http://www.brainyquote.com/quotes/authors/h/helen_keller_2.html>. [p. 39]

[17] Nielsen, Kim E. *Beyond the Miracle Worker.* Boston: Beacon Press, 2002. [p. 39]

[18] Saint Augustine. Thinkexist.com. Accessed 22 July 2010, <http://thinkexist.com/quotes/saint_augustine>. [p. 42]

[19] "Agape." *New World Encyclopedia.* 28 Aug 2008. Accessed 11 Aug 2010, <http://www.newworldencyclopedia.org/entry/Agape?oldid=793806>. [p. 45]

[20] Lewis, C. S. *A Grief Observed.* San Francisco: Harper Collins, 1961. [p. 53]

[21] Hitch, Kathy. "Broken Believer," *DVD: Live at the Rococo Theatre.* © Simple Grace 2008. [p. 54]

[22] Metz, Johann Baptist. *Faith in History and Society: Toward a Practical Fundamental Society.* New York, Seabury Press, 1980. [p. 54]

[23] Bauman, Dean L. "A Time to Die," *Whispers of His Word.* Kearney: Morris Publishing, 1997. [p. 56-57]

[24] Cripe, Dawn. "I Wanna Run," *Rescued and Restored,* 2010. [p. 59]

[25] Gaultiere, Bill, Ph.D. " 'Fear Not!' 365 days a year." ©2010. *Soul Shepherding.* Accessed 8 Aug 2010, <http://www.soulshepherding.org/2010/07/fear-not-365-days-a-year>. [p. 59]

[26] Nouwen, Henry. Quoted by Charles R. Ringma in *The Seeking Heart: A Journey with Henri Nouwen.* Brewster, Massachusetts: Paraclete Press, 2006. [p. 60]

[27] Vine, W.E. *Vine's Expository Dictionary of Old and New Testament Words.* Nashville: Thomas Nelson Publishers, 1984. [p. 64]

[28] Lingle, Mary. *Compassionate Friends Newsletter* 3, no.2 (April, May, June 2009). [p. 71]

[29] Kosmin, Barry A. and Keysar, Ariela. "American Religious Identification Survey (ARIS) 2008." Accessed 11 Aug 2010, <http://www.americanreligionsurvey-aris.org/reports/ARIS-Report_2008.pdf>. [p. 75]

[30] Saint Augustine. Quoted by Rev. Jay Sidebotham in "What Next?" © 2002 by St. Bartholomew's Church in the City of New York. Accessed 24 July 2010, <http://www.stbarts.org/old/ser051202.htm>. [p. 76]

[31] Nouwen, Henry. Quoted by Charles R. Ringma in *The Seeking Heart: A Journey with Henri Nouwen*. Brewster, Massachusetts: Paraclete Press, 2006. [p. 80]

[32] The Holy Bible, Conformable to the King James Version, Edition 1611. New York: The World Publishing Company. No copyright date available. [p. 82]

[33] Newman, John Henry. *Adam's Return: The Five Promises of Male Initiation*, © 2004. Quoted by Rowland Croucher and others, 19 Aug 2005, John Mark Ministries. Accessed 16 Aug 2010, <http://jmm.aaa.net.au/articles/15625.htm>. [p. 82]